The Martial Arts Parent's Frequently Asked Questions: How to Unlock Your Child's Potential Through Martial Arts

Grandmaster Ryan Andrachik has spent over 35 years studying and practicing martial arts. Established in 1994, his Asian Sun training centers form Ohio's largest martial arts school. Now Master Andrachik shares his hard-won knowledge and experience about how to make fitness and discipline part of your child's path to success, confidence, and happiness.

This easy-to-read book offers practical advice for parents, children, and martial artists of all ages and experience levels. Its honest discussions will help your family overcome the challenges we all face, whether we're aspiring Olympians or sixth graders who just want to make it through Wednesday.

These questions feature real-life examples from Asian Sun students.

From attitude to performance, this one-of-a-kind resource offers helpful hints that you can read in the lobby during a single martial arts class — but revisit, use, and refine over a lifetime.

table of contents

The Martial Arts Parent's Frequently Asked Questions: How to Unlock Your Child's Potential Through Martial Arts

by Grandmaster Ryan Andrachik
with David Ferris

Asian Sun Press
Hudson, Ohio

First edition. Originally published September 2014.

Asian Sun Press

5837 Darrow Rd., Hudson, Ohio 44236
United States

www.AsianSun.net
Facebook.com/AsianSunMartialArts • @Asian_Sun

Produced in conjunction with 6623 Press

Cover and graphics by Daniel Holmes

Cover photo of Vincie Ripepi and portrait of Victoria Ripepi
(p. 76) by Prestige Portraits (formerly Woodard Photographic)

Library of Congress Cataloging-in-Publication Data

Andrachik, Ryan and Ferris, David.

The Martial Arts Parent's Frequently Asked Questions: How
to Unlock Your Child's Potential Through Martial Arts / by
Ryan Andrachik, with David Ferris.

p. cm – (Asian Sun Martial Arts Series)

Paperback ISBN-13 978-0692284094 (pbk. ; alk. Paper)
Paperback ISBN-10 0692284095 (pbk. ; alk. Paper)

1. Martial Arts. 2. Taekwondo. 3. Parenting. 4. Sports.
5. Fitness. 6. Motivation. 7. Success. I. Title. II. Series.

about the author

Grandmaster Ryan Andrachik is a 7th degree black belt in Taekwondo, recognized by World Song Moo Kwan, Kukkiwon and USA Taekwondo.

He began studying martial arts at the age of 6. He was personally taught Taekwondo by Grandmaster Il Joo Kim, a 9th *dan* black belt. Andrachik earned his Muay Thai black belt from Grandmaster Bob Chaney.

In 1994, Andrachik established Asian Sun, which is now Ohio's largest martial arts school.

As Asian Sun's *Kwan Jang Nym* (head instructor), he is active in the Midwest martial arts community. His roles include USA Taekwondo Martial Arts Commissioner, Sports Chairman of Lake Erie Taekwondo, past United States Taekwondo Union (USTU) Ohio Taekwondo Association Secretary General, and past Regional Director of Amateur Athletic Union (AAU) Taekwondo Region 6.

Ryan Andrachik (right, 7th degree black belt) and son Vincie Ripepi (left, 5th degree) outside the United States Taekwondo Association training facility at the United States Olympic Training Center, before Ripepi's 2014 team tryout.

Master Andrachik has personally trained 28 master instructors (4th *dan* and higher black belts) and over 600 black belt Students, including six in his own home.

In 2014, he was inducted into the International Karate and Kickboxing Hall of Fame. He was nominated by Grandmaster Bob Chaney.

Says Chaney, "What separates Master Andrachik from other school owners is the positive attitude of his students, and his ability to produce many quality instructors, students, and fighters with excellent attitude."

David Ferris is an Ohio Society of Professional Journalists Best Reporter of the Year. He teaches at the University of Akron. He is a second degree black belt in Taekwondo. He and his wife study Muay Thai. Their daughters study Muay Thai and Taekwondo. One is a black belt. The other is close.

Notes regarding style, usage, and content:

Many common variations exist for the titles of martial arts. This book capitalizes all styles, for consistency, and in respect.

Photo images may reflect limitations in the source material.

Unless noted, the names of all minors and students have been changed to preserve their anonymity.

foreword

Parents start their children in martial arts for a variety of reasons. Some want discipline, focus, coordination, fitness, and more. But children receive all of these benefits from martial arts over time — *time* being the key focus.

As a father, I want my children to receive the same rewards I've received from martial arts. But my children do not possess the same drive and perseverance adults need to overcome challenges when trying to attain that goal. It takes time.

Ask yourself: Do you tackle challenges in your life now in the same way you did when you were 5? Of course you don't.

Questions posed in this book come directly from parents who attend our schools. We answer them every week. And every parent usually believes their struggles are unique. The reality is that every parent, at one time or another, faces these questions when engaging any long-term goal with their children.

I face them with my daughters. Sometimes parents assume my kids roll out of bed with the same passion for martial arts as I do, just because their dad runs a martial arts school. They don't. I have to remind, fight, and — sometimes, on rare occasions — bribe my five year old to go to class, like any other parent.

The difference is: After years of practice, I have personally experienced the powerful benefits. And I bring those skills to every challenge I face when studying — and teaching — martial arts.

Martial arts truly have changed my life, and it will do the same for your children.... If you bring them to class twice a week.

— **Steve Seyerle,**
   General Manager, Asian Sun Martial Arts
   3rd Dan, Taekwondo

introduction

I like manuals.

I read constantly. I want to be a better martial artist. I want to be a better business owner. I want to be the best parent I can be.

Even if we give our all every day, there is something we're not doing, something that we *could* be doing. Some little piece of knowledge could improve me. And it could help me help the people around me.

Sustained success doesn't happen by accident, regardless of how you define "success."

So I read books like Doug Lipp's *Disney U: How Disney University Develops the World's Most Engaged, Loyal, and Customer-Centric Employees*, Jack Welch's *Winning*, and Stephen R. Covey's *Habits* series. And I tell my staff about them in our weekly meetings. And the next week, I tell my instructors about new things I learned. And two

3

months later, I tell them about the old books again. Because I read them again. And this time, I learned a different lesson, because I had more experience.

That is the kind of book I wanted to write: one you can read, then read again later. And read again later. And read again. I hope it works for you.

No matter what you are doing, it is not enough to see something once. You need to absorb it. You need to be *ready* to hear it. And even if we understand it, something will distract us eventually. For most of us, only so much information fits in our head at once. It doesn't matter if you are studying plumbing, polymer science, or martial arts.

At Asian Sun, we call our style *Jin Bo Ryu* Martial Arts; it means "The Way of Success Through Continuous Improvement." No matter how talented you are, martial arts is not the kind of skill-set that you perfect. The sport changes. Our bodies change. Life changes. Martial arts help address the challenges the world throws at you, whether you are 6 or 60.

Martial art is my business. It is my life. It is a large part of my family life. I have owned a large martial arts school for 20 years now, and I still teach classes for students of all ranks. Over my 35 years of martial arts experience, with the help of friends, mentors, my family, and countless students, I have learned some lessons and acquired some knowledge. Here is some of it.

I visit all Asian Sun locations regularly. I attend our school's tournaments. Coaching my son, I travel to competitions all over the world. And every day, I talk to parents. Some are excited. Some are frustrated. Some drive their children to class and watch them from the lobby. Some study and spar alongside their kids. Some are experienced. Some are new to the world of martial arts.

No matter who they are, no matter where they are, parents all have the same goals: They want their child to do well. They want their child to be happy.

So parents have questions. Just as students have questions. And we have hundreds of students. My staff and I enjoy talking to all the people I can. But there are only so many instructors, and there is only so much time. We would like to spend an hour with every family every night, but sooner than later, someone has to be home to eat dinner, do homework, and get the kids to bed. So questions go unasked and unanswered.

With this short book, I hope to answer some of those questions. And with those answers, I hope I can provide a roadmap to success for martial arts parents and students — whether your definition of "success" means getting a good workout, boosting your child's confidence, or raising an aspiring champion.

These are the answers to the questions parents ask me the most. Some of them seem similar. But day after day, they resurface in these distinct forms.

So I believe the issues are worth examining from different angles. Consider them bonus questions.

I hope they help you.

And if they create more questions, please come see me. I don't know everything. But I have a lot of experience. Together, we can get you where you want to go.

— Master Instructor Ryan Andrachik

"The journey of a thousand miles
 begins with a single step."

— Lao Tzu

chapter 1

"How do I find a good martial arts school?"

Question:

"How do I find a good martial arts school?"

Answer:

Most people ask the wrong questions when they are looking for a martial arts school. When people call, the only question they ask is, "How much is it?"

That's the number one problem: They think shopping for a professional service is the same as calling for tires in a garage.

That's the most frustrating thing we go through. It happens every day. Where we live, prices are similar, from school to school. So should you settle for lesser quality to save a few dollars a month? I think not.

So when people call and ask for a price quote, we explain that the only way to understand it is to come in and see. People who are serious will come in. When we take calls, I can almost guarantee that we're the school closest to them. Or another school didn't answer the phone.

A parent's focus should be on finding a professional organization that cares about their children — not price. When a parent shops for

martial arts lessons, they are literally finding a private school for their child.

I understand the impulse. It's smart to shop around. But you can't judge a school by their ads or their Google ranking alone. Would you choose a preschool by calling around and getting tuition quotes? You have to actually go in and try it.

So as a potential customer, how do you judge a school?

What you really want to consider is a school's professionalism, your reaction, their honesty, and its overall convenience.

Professionalism:

Ask if they conduct background checks for their employees. We do. From amateur sports to the Olympics, that is an important new trend in coaching. And it's overdue, but it's great that more and more organizations do it.

Next, look at what kind of business it is.

Owners of martial arts schools should treat it like any other retail establishment. You have to meet the instructors. The school should be professional. When you go to Abercrombie and Fitch, do you see empty energy drink cans on the floor? You wouldn't go to a high school and see teachers running around in tattered shirts. Instructors should be dressed accordingly. They should have uniforms on. If they're neglecting things like cleanliness and appearance, what else are they neglecting?

Whether you're looking for a fitness activity or a lifestyle, if we're considering martial arts, we're talking about an activity that can have a great impact on your life. You're going to have to dedicate two or more nights a week to driving your child to a school, for years. So it has to be convenient.

But at the same time, there's usually more than one school around. A bigger school will not necessarily be better. And a smaller school will not necessarily be better. **Go visit them. Be reasonable, but don't go looking for the right price alone. Consider how you feel about the school.**

Your Reaction:

Meeting the instructor is important. And not only that: You have to let your child participate in a class. You have to watch what they're doing. You have to make sure your child likes the instructor. And hopefully, the instructor seems interested in teaching your child.

Try to find a place that offers a trial program that is free or $10 or $20.

And if you decide you like it, then enroll. If you're afraid of commitment, sign up for a smaller course, maybe six months. Then even if your child doesn't like it, say she gives you a hard time, make her complete it anyway. Because now you're teaching the value of a work ethic. You complete the course. And that's the whole point: Your child learns to follow through.

So a good school will give you a trial period. Take it. **See if you like it.**

Before you interview a school, ask yourself why you're there. What are you looking for? What results do you want?

Parents are all looking for the same things: They want their children to be safe. They want them to learn. They want them to improve.

We always ask, "What is the reason you're getting your child involved?" We'll hear "focus," "discipline," "getting in shape," or "My child has special needs," or "We're struggling with A.D.H.D."

Many parents have goals when they enroll a child. Here's what you probably don't realize: No matter what you want, your child is going to get it all. We teach a traditional martial art. And the benefits are the same, regardless of a student's goals, whether we're working with a 10-year-old girl who lacks confidence, a 14-year-old boy who has trouble focusing, or a 36-year-old woman who wants to lose weight.

You can't study a martial art and just get *some* of the benefits. You can't come to Taekwondo classes and just improve your balance.

The reason we ask is so *you*, the parent, understand the reasons why you're bringing your children to our school. It's not just an activity. It's not baseball. It's not soccer. (Though having clearly defined goals can only help maximize your benefits from other activities, as well.)

As a parent, maybe you want to improve your daughter's ability to focus. So we'll tell you, "OK, so you understand: It's not an overnight deal. It's going to take some time. You'll see some results right away. And then you'll see no results for a little bit. And then you'll see a surge of results — in time." And that's not the most persuasive thing for me to tell you when I own a company and I'm trying to get you to enroll as a student. But it's the truth.

Honesty:

The next thing you need to look for is *honesty*.

Don't be swayed by the magic number of a price. And don't be swayed by promises.

Some martial arts schools are big on promising quick-and-easy results. I can't teach you anything in five easy lessons. You can't take a Saturday seminar and suddenly become bully-proof for the rest of your life. Parents want to have their daughter take one self-defense class before they go to college. Realistic, practical self-defense doesn't work like that.

That's the thing about martial arts: It can be an activity. It can be fun. But to get results, to be good at anything, you're going to need to dedicate some time to it.

So if all martial arts — if taught properly and professionally — have the same benefits, then what makes a school right for you?

Convenience:

Take a close look at the schedule. You need a school where, if you can't make it one day, you can go another day. I have been involved in this industry for 24 years, and I can tell you: Schedules change. Your child will want to play baseball. They *will* want to go to a friend's birthday party. Your school should have a flexible schedule that can accommodate you if you need it to.

I told you to take your gut reaction into account. **It's also important to take into account how your child feels.** Don't let their first reaction be the only determining factor in your choice. But note it carefully. Maybe they will love the school. Maybe they won't.

Other factors will affect the atmosphere. If your child is young, if they're having a bad day, maybe they won't enjoy the first class. Maybe they're tired. Maybe they're hungry. Maybe you pulled them away from their video game. If your child has a negative reaction, but your adult instincts tell you it's a good school, maybe "I don't like it!" isn't your son's final answer.

At all of our schools, we give students a 30-day trial period. If they're really on the fence about it, we say, "Let's bring them back and try again." If they don't like it the second time, then it might not be the right activity for them at this age.

The first lesson is important. For both of you. You should watch the first lesson. You can tell what your child is reacting to. And you can see if the instructor is really interested in reaching your child.

So back to everybody's reflexive first concern: The budget usually isn't really an issue.

Does your child like the classes? If the answer is "no," then all your other questions are irrelevant.

Does he like the instructor? If it's "no," stop there.

Is there a trial period? If your child lasts three classes, you're set. They'll have no problems at all.

Case Study:

A mother brought her three-year-old son to one of our schools. The mother looked disheveled and stressed. She had his sister with him. It was obvious she had to get the daughter someplace else, and that the son was the source of stress. I started explaining our free 30-day trial membership. And halfway through, she gave me a credit card, and she took the daughter to the dance school next door. She basically said, "Please fix him," and left Josh crying in my lobby.

Josh cried all the way through every lesson for a month. He kept crying, and the mother kept bringing him. When it didn't get better, the mother wanted to take him out of classes.

After the third class, a lot of martial arts schools would have said, "He's not ready yet. Bring him back in a year." Eventually, we designated an assistant instructor to stick close to Josh for all of his classes.

Josh was a challenge. But eventually, he stopped crying. Things got better. And over the next seven years, he became one of our success stories. I recently saw him outside of class, at a community event. He was a confident, charismatic leader, with a trail of kids following him around. There is no doubt his mother found the right martial arts school.

The patience and resolve of our instructors helped change that child's life.

Every school offers the same benefits. Every school claims they're the best. Every school has a program. But how dedicated are they to meeting your needs? What will they do to help you?

Here's what sets a good school apart from a great one: If your child is having problems, are the instructors willing to spend extra time with them? The one thing they can't fake is how much time and effort they will put in.

chapter 2

"My child is having a bad day and doesn't want to go to class. What should I do?"

Question:

"My child is having a bad day and doesn't want to go to class. What should I do?"

Answer:

Some days, your child will not want to go to class. Should you make them go to class? What can you do to change their mind? If you let them skip a class, are you destroying their routine and creating a confusing inconsistency?

Here's what people fail to realize. And it makes all the difference when you're incorporating martial arts into your daily life.

You have to prepare your child to go to class, just like you have to prepare yourself to go to work.

Let's say a child is being stubborn and doesn't want to go to class today. It usually has nothing to do with martial arts. It usually has everything to do with what you're doing before class, and with how you're preparing them before class.

Speaking as a parent who has to take his children to class: If my kids' class starts at 6:30, we're not watching TV at 6:10. That will be a nightmare, trying to pull them away from that.

My young children, they're into Scooby-Doo right now. Scooby-Doo will beat martial arts team practice any day. With young kids, if they're watching TV right before they leave for class, they will never want to go. My older son, if he was playing video games, or he had friends over before class, class would always lose to his friends.

We also try to arrive at class 15 minutes early, to get a separation between everything else and class. I think that's important. Don't pull them away from whatever else they're doing and get them to class at the last second. We make sure, 15 minutes before we leave, they're not doing *anything* interesting. **Before you leave, disengage them well in advance.**

Routine is important. At our schools, you *can* go six days a week. But it's important not to shuffle the days you attend around. If you go Tuesday-Thursday or Monday-Wednesday, stick to it. This way, you're teaching your child about *doing what is expected.*

Sometimes, your child gets off the bus, and she's crying, and she's already complaining about not wanting to go to class. If that happens once a month and you miss class that day, it is not the end of the world. In that case, it is not martial arts that has caused today's problem. In a way, it's good if they step off the bus and say, "I don't want to go to class today" — because now you know they understand that today is martial arts day.

When it happens:

For achievers and type-A parents, the default mindset says you always have to stick to your routine, no matter what. But life will find a way to get in the way.

Skipping one day is not going to destroy your progress. You can look at your son and say, "I'm tired. I know you're tired. We're going to make a pact that we're going Thursday."

Schedule a make-up day. And then you stick to that. It's important to adhere to a routine. But it's also important to learn how to adapt; life has a way of deviating from your careful, reasonable plans.

But if you think you can get your child to class, then it's on us, the instructors. The instructors may not be part of the problem, but they can very well be the solution.

If you bring your child there, it's our job to make it fun. Don't be afraid to take the instructor aside and say, "We're having a hard time right now; is there anything you can do?" And at a good school, the instructor will always oblige. Always. And at my schools, they'd better oblige. If you go to Montrose and tell Master Pearlman, "Ryley is having a hard time today," then he'll be sure to highlight her in class and make her feel rewarded for her effort.

If a student can make that mental pivot over the course of a class — if she can go from having a bad day to having a good day, and a good workout is part of it, that's a powerful new association for them.

Here's an issue that people worry about:

From an instructor's point of view, do you look bad if you miss a class?

If you are going twice a week, we would rather see you twice a week than once per week. If you miss two or three weeks, we're glad to have you back — but we'd rather have seen you once in those two or three weeks. It just helps the consistency.

You need to understand, though: Unlike soccer or basketball, martial arts is not an activity that you can do for a season, then walk away from it for five months, then come back. If you and your kids get out of the habit of going, everything you worked for is undone. Sometimes, you will have more time to devote to it. Sometimes, you will have more enthusiasm. Regardless, it is important that you keep coming. You need to get your children to class at least once a week.

What if *you're* having a bad day?

Parents have bad days, too. We're human. Your third grader might disagree, but your day might have been far worse than theirs was. You *are* going to have those bad days.

The martial arts lifestyle is like exercising or eating healthy: Everyone's going to have a cheat day. Everyone's going to have that piece of cheesecake. But if you continue to have cheesecake every day, you're going to have problems.

Case Study:

We have a brown belt. He's been with us nearly three years. The family used to come to class five days a week. He came to every special event. Then, suddenly, his mother told us, "I can't get him to come to class any more."

Well, it turns out the problem is: He has been there every day for two years.

Then he discovered football. Now he would rather do football. It's new. It's exciting. So we needed to let him know he can do both.

When we tell families that they can come to "unlimited" classes, we mean they can come to almost any class, any time, as long as it's for an appropriate belt level. For most students, two days a week is optimum, based on their goals and needs. If they do six days a week, they *will* get burned out.

So now, during football season, he comes to class on Saturday. And when the season is over, he's on a twice-a-week schedule.

Everybody needs space.

That's a natural dynamic that happens to everyone. Sometimes you don't want to go.

The important thing is: You keep coming back.

"Focus is so important. I can teach you almost anything, but if you're not listening, you cannot learn."

— Asian Sun Master Instructor Bill Barnick

chapter 3

"My child's enthusiasm for martial arts is not blossoming into a real passion. Should we pursue it?"

Question:

"My child's enthusiasm for martial arts is not blossoming into a real passion. Should we pursue it?"

Answer:

If you're reading this, you probably want martial arts to be an important part of your child's life. We both know the benefits of martial arts.

Your child may have other ideas about it.

As a parent, you often need to coax your child through things they don't want to do. Sometimes it's homework. Sometimes it's chores. Sometimes it's Taekwondo. You can't plan every aspect of your child's life, but successful parents have goals for their children, whether they're specific or abstract.

Given our family's vocation and lifestyle, having the children active in martial arts is important. It literally keeps the family close together — we are all in the same place, working on similar things, together.

And we bond through a common interest and activity. My wife and I are fortunate that our children embrace the challenge. We don't pursue Taekwondo to the point of exclusion. All our children are black belts. We haven't forced any of them to study martial arts — but at various points, my wife and I have needed to actively lead them down the path.

Our youngest girls are 10 and 9 years old. I want them to be able to play golf. Because, say you work for any professional organization, very likely, it will have some kind of golf outing in the summertime. If you can't golf, you're excluded from it. You don't have to be good. But you have to know the rules and know how to play. If you can't do that, you have shut yourself out. So my girls will know how to golf. They don't have to love it.

And they're going to know how to bowl. In this part of the country, commonly, bowling is a popular social activity. I don't want them to miss an opportunity because they can't bowl. But golf and bowling aren't their first choices for how they want to spend an afternoon.

Here's the common thread: You want your child to develop a skill. But she might not need it for years. And practicing it is outside her interests. So you need to do what you can to make her want to do it. There always has to be a carrot involved, a reward system, an enticing offer to lead them through.

Martial arts is set up as a reward system. A student who comes to class is rewarded with stripes on their belt. And the stripes accumulate as their skills develop. When they have enough stripes — when they have made enough progress — they are allowed to test for their next belt. As they move from belt to belt, they are working on receiving a positive incentive: in this case, a black belt.

Case Study:

Our young daughters don't always want to spend a Saturday afternoon sweating at a team practice. But they know if they do it, they'll see some friends at practice, and they will end up having fun. They know once they're done working, maybe later they will be able to do something that is 100% recreational. And that's fun. You work now, you play later.

The girls are both black belts. The journey to this level was definitely made easier with the use of incentives. It's not bribery. It's a reward. And that's how life works: If you work harder and you put in more time, you get more. The girls put in more time than they necessarily want to — and they see it improve their perceived quality of life.

chapter 4

"Some of the students at my son's belt level look better or worse than he does. Should he be at a different rank?"

Question:

"Some of the students at my son's belt level look better than he does. Are they better, or is he worse? Does the school have him at the right rank?"

Answer:

This is a really, really important issue.

I talk about this all the time: For example, parents ask me constantly, "What is 'black belt'"? Black belt is something different for everyone.

That's what people who aren't teachers don't understand: **Especially for children, there is no constant.**

The best thing about martial arts is that it is a personal journey. It isn't about everyone being the same. It is about your own self-improvement.

So if you try to take a hardline approach and say, "You're not good enough for this belt," then you're missing the point. You need to build their confidence level to the point where they can be that good. Then you can build the body after that.

Now, with the confident kids, you've got to build the technique first. And then the mind will follow the technique. You have to understand what martial arts are. And you have to understand what the belts represent.

Martial arts schools plan their whole curriculum around belt tests. I know if you miss two belt tests, you're probably going to quit. Statistically, if you miss two tests in a row, you're gone, because you don't feel like you're making any progress. Belt tests keep the students going.

The rank is not the most important thing in martial arts; it's the time. But you can't just tell people, "Put in ten years, and you'll eventually get a yellow belt." For kids — and, often adults, there's no reward if there's not a goal in sight.

That's why college is so hard: You need to be self-motivated. And there's no reward for making it through two or three years. This is why a nine-year-old cannot handle college. And if your black belt is eight years away, it's hard to stay focused on that goal.

The way I see it, the belts are not only to designate rank, but to keep you going. Because I can get you to be good over time. I can't make you great in six months or a year. I can make you better. But if you quit, I can't make you better, ever.

If you're watching your eight-year-old purple belt and comparing her to a 12-year-old who is more coordinated, maybe you will think, "Oh, my eight-year-old doesn't belong here." But flip it. Let's say you have an uncoordinated 12-year-old, and she's testing next to an 8-year-old who's a star member of a championship soccer team, a gifted kid who was going to be good at any sport. Maybe the eight-year-old kid looks way better, but you can't judge it like that.

Mentally and physically, look at your child now, and look at your child six months from now. And I guarantee the results: She will be better. That's what you're here for: You want to be a better version of yourself.

Don't worry about the other students' skill level and progress. Concentrate on yours.

Case Study:

I had a student who was 45 years old.

He was terrible. Terrible. And not because he didn't have potential. But his life was very complicated on every level: his family, his business, and other stresses that would weigh on anybody. His Taekwondo was scattered, but so was his mind.

He would throw a technique. Then he would rethink it. Then he would readjust his stance. Every single move. He was always trying to see everything from every possible angle. And because he was having so much difficulty outside the school, it carried into his Taekwondo.

So his art was not good. But this guy needed Taekwondo; he needed an outlet so he could work on concentrating elsewhere in his life.

At his blue belt test, it took him several tries to do his board break. When I was tying his belt around him, he tried to give it back to me. He said, "Sir, I don't deserve this."

I ended the conversation very quickly. I said, "Sir, this is my school. I've been teaching for over 20 years. Are you telling me that you don't deserve it, based on your experience and your expert opinion? You need to trust me."

Was he as good as other blue belts? No. But he was improving. In time, he got better. And in time, he became good. Most importantly, he came to class, and because of that his son came to class. He did not realize it at the time, but he was not practicing martial arts for him — he was practicing for his son.

You cannot base your progress on the best person in the room. Every person is an individual.

The Andrachik family, August 2014, with Master Andrachik's teacher, Grandmaster Il Joo Kim, 9th Dan Kukkiwon, 9th Dan Song Moo Kwan (center).

A favorite motivational quote from Master Instructor Norman Kim:

"We are what we repeatedly do. Excellence, therefore, is not an act, but a habit."

— Aristotle

"A confident person can do
 anything. We teach confidence."

— Master Barnick

chapter 5

"My child is being bullied. Can you help?"

Question:

"My child is being bullied. Can you help?"

Answer:

You can teach your child to handle a bully. We can help. But it takes time. You need to understand that.

Bullying is a hot topic right now. I have some experience with it.

I am an only child. As a child, I was bullied constantly.

I was bullied, in part, because I didn't have an older brother to push me around, or a younger brother to fight with. So I went to school, and someone pushed me, and I was bewildered.

I didn't understand it. As anyone would be, I was overwhelmed, standing there stunned, thinking, "Why would you do that to me?" I didn't get it.

Once a bully hits you, and they get away with it, in the mind of both the bully and the victim, this is the norm. A pattern has been established. I'm not saying it's right. But you need to understand the psychological dynamics that factor into a bullying situation.

In that scenario, you didn't stand up for yourself. Just like I didn't stand up for myself. So the bully is going to do it again and again. And again. And again. They have no incentive to stop.

Then maybe the victim speaks up about it eventually.

The dad says, "You need to stand up for yourself."

Well, now it's too late. You let it go for how long? And if you stand up for yourself and they shut you down, now you're right back in the same position.

Bullying is not a dynamic that can be tackled in an afternoon or a weekend. You're not going to do it. It's going to take a long time, because you need to make the child confident enough. And *then* you have to be able to get the child to back it up. **Because the thing about bullying is this: It could end up in scuffle. It can happen.**

There are all these one-day classes that claim to teach your child how to stop being bullied. We offer seminars, but we don't charge for them, in large part because it's not that easy.

That's why we don't advertise with flyers that say, "Stop your child from being bullied in one afternoon!" **Because the truth is: There is no quick fix.**

The damage has been done over how many months or years? You can't fix it overnight. You have to build the child up. It's a gradual process. So as the child gets stronger and more confident, the skills increase.

If you focus on turning your kid into a bruiser, it won't help. If you focus on turning your child into a leader, it will. Bullies don't pick on leaders.

We're not saying you've got to fight the kid. But if they push you, and you say "Cut it out," and they push you again, *now* what are you going to do? And if you don't do anything, now you reinforce the position that the bully is dominant.

What if you tell your child, "Stand up for yourself" or "Hit him back"? Then, what if the bully hits *your* child back *four* times? Now what? Your child is getting his butt kicked. You told him to stick up for himself, and now you made the situation worse.

That's what happened to me. That's how I got into martial arts. I was on my own. I had to learn to stand up for myself. And make it stick.

Parents say, "Well, just ignore them."

OK, let's see how that's going to work. Sometimes that works. But more often, they keep picking on you. If you have a problem with a co-worker, do you just ignore it? Or do you assemble some kind of strategic action plan?

There are all kinds of bullying. There's the verbal kind, too. Boys face it. Girls face it. And it's the same, no matter whether we're talking about school or college or work.

But it's all about having the confidence to be able to deal with it.

Case Study:

The best parent in the world may have a blind spot as to why their child is being bullied.

One of our students came to us because he was being bullied. His dad is a big, outspoken man, with a bigger personality. The family is not originally from America. So when his dad speaks, he has a distinct manner, and it comes through as a colorful, exotic accent.

For the son, it didn't work as well. He was young. He didn't have a full command of the language. He didn't have the verbal skills his dad did. So, to his peers, he was The Quiet Kid. He didn't want to speak, and he couldn't speak out. And that led to him being picked on.

So his parents brought him to us. They said, "He doesn't have confidence."

In class, right off the bat, he was amazing. As time went on, he only got better. And when he broke the boards in his yellow belt test, all of a sudden, martial arts was the only thing he could talk about. With every test, his confidence grew.

When someone tried to put him down, now he had the confidence to stand up for himself — and he had the skills to back it up.

The bullying stopped, but it took time.

Ryan Andrachik (left), at his 2014 Karate and Kickboxing Hall of Fame induction, with Grandmaster Bob Chaney (right).

"The secret to getting a black belt?
 Coming to class."

— Master Barnick

chapter 6

"My child wants to quit.
Should we let him?"

Question:

"My child wants to quit. Should we let him?"

Answer:

Students usually want to quit for a few different reasons. And letting them quit isn't the best way to handle any of them. Let's look at four common scenarios.

Scenario 1: "I don't want to."

Usually, the problems with "My child doesn't like it any more" have nothing to do with martial arts. We look at a student's attendance card, and he hasn't been there for two months. That's when we know it's a problem.

As parents, sometimes we overlook our role in our children's performance. Sometimes, this can be the scenario: A child's interest drops, and the parent has inadvertently contributed to it.

We all want our kids to be happy. We don't want to make them unhappy. So here's what happens:

It's the end of the school year, the kids are busy, they have birthday parties, they're tired, all their friends are having a water-balloon battle outside.

They ask if they can please, please, *please* skip class. Now they haven't been to class this week. Now they go to soccer camp for a week. Now the family goes on vacation. Now they haven't been to class for a month.

You need to get them to class. But it's the middle of summer, and the neighborhood kids are all outside having a blast. So, now, they have to miss the fun, and go to class. And what do you get?

"I don't want to do it any more."

In this case, the interest has faltered, in part, because you haven't followed your schedule. You said you were going to do it Mondays and Wednesdays. And you haven't done it. Now, in their head, the norm is not "I go to class Monday and Wednesday." In their head, the norm is, "I don't go to class, and class interrupts my social agenda."

It's not always easy, but if you commit to keeping your child on a regular schedule, you're less likely to have The Quitting Conversation.

Scenario 2: "It's too hard."

In many a martial arts career, there does come a point where it feels like moving forward is more trouble than it's worth. When you are learning a new form that consists of 88 motions, maybe it's not enough to go to class once or twice a week, and you should be practicing at home, but you're not.

Then you go to class, and you're not where you want to be, and it's frustrating. Or, physically, you are not where you want to be, and its affecting your mechanics. Now the struggle doesn't feel like it's worth it.

Maybe all the kids in your son's Monday-Wednesday class are on the competition sparring team, and he's not, so sparring has become a source of frustration.

Whatever the challenge, it boils down to the same thing: "It's too hard. I don't want to do it. I want to quit."

Talk to your instructor, whatever the problem is. It doesn't always have to be a parents-versus-child conflict. If your child says a form is "too hard," maybe a one-on-one lesson will make the form more clear in your daughter's mind. Whatever the obstacle is, a break from the routine might help identify the problem and move past it.

Scenario 3: "I don't like it anymore."

What if your child is a red belt who says she doesn't like it any more? They're one or two belts away from black belt, and they want to stop. Or they say they want to stop "for now," and they *promise* they'll come back to it later.

Everybody in life needs a carrot, some positive promise to keep them moving forward. Then the horse is going to chase the prize. So what's the reward here? What can you do to help give them an incentive to remain engaged?

Talk to your instructor. Black belt is such an awesome achievement that quitting may be something they regret later in life.

And maybe a reward won't be enough. Maybe it requires some firm parental leadership on your part.

When you enroll in a school, you are paying for the service of a martial arts education. When a student earns a black belt, that is a *degree*, not unlike an academic degree.

If your son really, really doesn't like it, that's a conversation you need to have with your instructor. You need to identify *why* they don't like it.

So you find out: Maybe they think class is boring.

Well, what exactly do they think is boring? Now you can address the problem.

If they're "just not into it," whatever they've been doing in class, then what *are* they into?

If they like weapons, you can concentrate on weapons.

If they like breaking, maybe you can work on an exciting breaking routine for a test.

If they like sparring, they can focus on training for an inter-school tournament.

Or maybe the school offers a junior referee training program.

Or maybe if your daughter doesn't like breaking and sparring, the school has a forms team.

Maybe going through the regular drills feels more productive if you're focused on winning gold in an upcoming tournament.

If they don't like any of that, find something else. In martial arts, there is something for everybody.

Scenario 4: "*Really*, I'm not into it any more."

So maybe your daughter *still* wants to quit. Or you have a green belt who says, "Well, I'm just not into it any more."

As a parent, if I have a child who is a year and a half away from their black belt, I would figure out ways that I can keep them interested. A black belt is forever. You can put that on your child's college application. You can put that on their adult résumé. Schools and employers don't just want to see a 3.94 grade point average. They want to see achievements.

So *why* is she not into it? What are you doing as a parent, or what are your instructors doing as an organization that's making the class a negative experience? You're so close; you're right there.

As an organization, we can ask, "Well, *why* did a student lose interest?"

In this case, students want to quit for one of three reasons:

1. They have an inconsistent schedule.

2. They're doing something else right now that you're trying to pull them away from. Often, kids don't think long-term. They think if they suddenly commit to never doing it again, if they say they quit, then they can stay home and finish this level on their video game, and spend the rest of their life playing and having a good time.

3. They had a bad experience in class. Maybe sparring went badly, and they were hit harder than they were comfortable with, or just surprised by a stiff blow. And now they're scared. Or maybe an instructor corrected them. Or maybe you corrected them. It can be, literally, the fight-or-flight response. They don't want to fight. So the alternative instinct says, "Get out of there!"

So it's important to have a discussion. Instead of…

"I don't want to!"

"Well, you're going to!"

…you want to have a discussion. Talk about it. Identify what the issue is and work through it. And a lot of the time, we can get them back in, and get them to black belt.

We have great success when the student isn't in it alone.

Some parents study with their children. In that case, there's not a lot of choice: Mom says, "I'm going; are *you* ready to go?"

Would my older children have reached the levels they did if I had just driven them to the school, dropped them off, picked them up, and maybe asked how class went? Probably not.

I review this with my staff all the time: When was the last time a student came in and said, "I quit. I'm done?" They don't.

When students quit, they fall off. It's gradual. I have never had a brown belt come and say, "Sir, I'm quitting, you can take this belt." They just don't show up for class. Then they don't show up for another couple months. Why did they stop attending? There's some motivation that's not there.

If you want your child to take classes, but she doesn't want to, what can you do to make her more comfortable?

What can you offer to make your child realize the value of this commitment?

What can the instructors do to make classes more inviting or attractive? They should be able to do something.

Remember the initial goal. Achieve it.

Case Study:

This one story about Master Bill Barnick, who is one of our head instructors. When he was a child, he wanted to quit. It was a learning experience for both of us.

When his mom enrolled him, he was 12, and he needed help with his confidence.

It was going well — to start with. But at the time, when you joined, you didn't need sparring pads until you were a blue belt. Between starting and reaching blue belt, that was around a year.

So when it came to his blue belt, he wanted to quit — because he didn't want to spar. But it took some time for him to tell anybody that. We didn't know exactly what the issue was. His mom just knew he wanted to quit.

(He wasn't the only student that happened with. Now you get the sparring equipment the first week.)

Master Barnick's mom wouldn't let him quit. In time, we coaxed an explanation out of him. And we showed him he wasn't going to get beat up. After that bump in the road, he achieved his initial goals, set new ones, and continued growing.

"Don't think about what can go wrong;
think about what can go right."

— Asian Sun Master Instructor
and Competition Team Coach
Vincie Ripepi

From fan to competition: Asian Sun's Vincie Ripepi with Taekwondo icon Steven Lopez. Above: Ripepi at age 12 (left) and Lopez (right). Below: Ripepi at age 18 (left), with Lopez (right), after sparring at USA Taekwondo National Team trials in 2014.

"We learn martial arts as helping weakness. You never fight for people to get hurt. You're always helping people."

— Jackie Chan

chapter 7

"How can I get my child to be more assertive?"

Question:

"How can I get my child to be more assertive?"

Answer:

There's always a "How do I….?" question. The answer is "time and practice." For all of them. That's all there is: time and practice.

Time and practice solve it all: Flexibility. Developing a better axe kick. Cardio conditioning. Physical speed. Mental toughness.

"How do I get my child to be more assertive?" is a popular one with members of our competition team. You can tell your child to be more aggressive all day long. And until they actually practice, they're not going to do it.

You perform how you practice. If you're going to give a speech, you practice giving the speech in front of a mirror. You deliver in situations that simulate a real performance. If you want your child to be more aggressive, maybe you get a heavy bag and practice *attacking* it for 30 seconds. You practice being more aggressive. **Talking about it doesn't do much, if anything. You have to practice it.**

Sometimes you need outside help and the right kind of reinforcement.

We have a team member. He's an early teenager. He needs to start kicking faster. He's at a level now where he absolutely wants the truth. He won't get anywhere if we just pat him on the back and say, "Great! You look good." For him, you need to say, "You need to kick faster…. No, *faster…. No, faster*. If you don't push harder, you're not going to get better."

And it's hard, because at that point, at age 13, he's going to get better, or he's going to quit. **If you want to be successful, eventually, it's going to get hard, no matter what you do.** So this is a great life lesson now for him.

Because he's at the level where he's coachable, and I can be harder on him, and he can respond. He'll have more respect for what I'm saying, because I'm telling him the truth. He may not like to hear what I'm telling him, but he'll respect it. So that's where we work on their confidence. And when he kicks well, we tell him "Great!" But that's because he did it right.

He needs to hear some positive feedback, and he needs to hear negative feedback. It's a fantasy to believe that if you just keep saying "Great, great, great, you're super," that he'll perform at an elite level.

Nobody intentionally practices something the wrong way. Especially in competition, in the middle of a workout, most people don't think they're not giving it everything they have. Beyond areas that are black-and-white, when you get into competitive performance, you need that feedback.

If we're working on you being aggressive, you think that you are attacking the bag as hard as you can — but to me, you might look lethargic.

If we're working on flexibility, you may think you're kicking at head height, but I might see that your feet are only coming up to chest level.

This happens all the time: We drill students to keep their hands up and protect their head. During a fight, I say, "HANDS UP!" And the hands go up. And 30 seconds later, they're down at your chest again. You're not dropping your hands because you're lazy. It just happens. It happens to the best people in the world. You believe you're doing what we practiced. But you're not, and you don't realize it.

You need an outside perspective from someone you trust.

Everybody can benefit from a push — the right kind of push.

Case Study:

One of our team members just won a gold medal at the USA Taekwondo National Championships. We knew he could get there. We weren't always sure he would. His whole career in martial arts has been a roller coaster.

He would do well in a tournament. Then he would lose in the next one. Then he did well in the next. Then he lost. Then he did well at Nationals. Then he went to an open championship and was destroyed. He wasn't confident. He wasn't aggressive.

He had everything going for him: He's from a great family. The parents take classes with him, and they're great athletes. He had all the potential in the world, but we just couldn't get him to push harder. He's a teenage boy, so sometimes it was hard to tell him anything and get him to *listen*, to really believe what you were telling him. And there was nothing *wrong* with him; most teenage boys are like that.

So for the last couple years, it was a constant challenge. We knew what he needed to do. He knew what he needed to do. And it just never sank in. The practices could be tough, because, as instructors, we were repeating ourselves, saying the same things over and over again, telling him all the same things we told him last week. We knew it was just a matter of time until something changed inside him.

Then this year, at Nationals, everything clicked. He was doing everything we ever told him, and it all came together at the same time. He was pushing hard, really going after his opponents. He took down everybody in his path. And now he is a national gold medalist.

You can't make every single adjustment immediately, whether you're working on something physical or mental. It can be an issue about attitude, skill, or ability. The instructor wants it. The student wants it. The parent's biggest responsibility is to keep the carrot in front of your child, to keep them coming to class.

Set a goal. Work on it. It takes time.

"I wasn't any good at it right
 away, so I quit."

— Bart Simpson

"Never forget that, at the most, the teacher can give you fifteen percent of the art. The rest you have to get for yourself, through practice and hard work. I can show you the path, but I can not walk it for you."

— Master Tan Soho Tin

chapter 8

"Our gear stinks. How do we keep it fresh and clean?"

Question:

"Our gear stinks. How do we keep it fresh and clean?"

Answer:

The laundry issue is simple: You have one uniform for every day your child goes to class.

It's an expense, but if you go to class four days a week, and you just have one uniform, you're destroying it.

But if you just go to a family class and get a light workout twice a week, a regular uniform and regular laundry care should take care of it. If you're sweating gallons, however, your uniforms and equipment require some extra maintenance.

For the uniforms, our family just uses detergent in a regular wash.

With gear, the biggest thing is: You've got to get it out of that bag as soon as possible.

In the spring, it gets warmer outside. After class, you're all sweaty. You put the uniform in the trunk. It's hot outside. You wind up baking it. That's where all your problems start.

Get it out. Get it home as fast as possible. Open the bag. Air is important.

We let all our equipment sit out every night, so it dries off. If my gear is really sweaty, I'll wipe it down.

People have different methods.

With sparring pads, you can, technically, put them in a freezer for 24 hours. And that kills the microbes that cause the smell. It sounds like an urban legend, but it does work.

Some people like to let theirs sit out in the sun, but there's bacteria on there, and then you're baking the bacteria into the pads.

Some of our students carry a container of antiseptic wipes and thoroughly wipe down their gear after every class.

Our Daedo chest guards never smell, because we spray them with sanitizer that will kill anything. When Vincie and I and the guys train during the day, sweat is rolling off of the chest guards in buckets.

Regardless of what level you work out at, here's a neat trick: Put three or four dryer sheets in your bag. And by the time you get it home, it really won't smell so bad.

Febreze Sport works extremely well, too.

Case Study:

You need to take care of your gear, but you need to realize: It doesn't last forever.

A set of shin guards will last me about six months. And I train three, four times a week. It's definitely a wear item. If you take two 45-minute classes a week, your shin guards will last a long time. But if you're fighting three or four times a week, they'll take a beating.

Arm guards will last me nine to ten months. Head gear lasts a long time. It's easy to wipe down.

Any time any odor starts to cling to my gear, it's time to replace it. It's like shoes: When you have shoes that start to smell, you can try to put a Band-Aid on it and cover it, but that doesn't eliminate the problem.

"For me, the martial arts is a search for something inside. It's not just a physical discipline."

— Brandon Lee

"Just work hard and have the
   right attitude."

— Duke Roufus

chapter 9

"My school doesn't compete. How do I get them to give us what we need?"

Question:

"My school doesn't compete. How do I get them to give us what we need?"

Answer:

Talk to them about it.

Let's say your school doesn't compete.

If your school doesn't compete, and you really want to compete, I would have a conversation with the head instructor. And tell them your intention. Maybe it's possible they'll start a competition team for you. But honestly, most instructors are too busy with their current classes, or they have another job on the side, so they don't want to compete.

If your school doesn't compete nationally, and you want to, you're probably in the wrong school. You need to find a competitive program.

Or the odds are your instructor knows someone who has a competitive team that they can refer you to. Maybe you can take regular classes with your instructor, and take your competition classes at the school your instructor recommends. We've had a lot of people come to our classes over the years, from an hour away, two hours away. We're on good terms with the other instructors.

If you want to compete locally, that is usually much easier to arrange. But if your instructor is dead-set against it, you're probably at the wrong school. That doesn't make it a bad school; you have different priorities.

We are primarily a Taekwondo-oriented school, but if somebody wants to grapple, we're going to send them to a school that has a grappling program. If my students want to practice a style where they punch to the face, I would send them to our Muay Thai classes. If our Muay Thai students feel they don't get enough ring experience, our instructor will look for a local scrimmage or interschool match to get them the additional ring time they are seeking. That will get you more ring experience.

Whether the extra dimension you want is competitive forms, or weapons, or sparring, the questions are:

What do you want?

What is the problem?

If you're not getting it, how can you?

How can we help you learn what you want?

Your school is there to help you.

"It's not where you started in life — it's where you end up. Believe in yourself."

— Master Instructor Victoria Ripepi

chapter 10

"I want my children to learn martial arts, and I know it would be a good thing for them. But they don't want to take classes. Should I make them?"

Question:

"I want my children to learn martial arts, and I know it would be a good thing for them, for fitness or self defense. But they don't want to take classes. Should I *make* them?"

Answer:

That's a million-dollar question. It's basically the same as "I can't get my child to come" or "They're losing interest."

And it's common. For whatever reason, a parent knows the benefits of martial arts. And they want their children to learn. Some parents have a black belt. Or they have prior experience and wish they had completed their degree.

Kids should know how to defend themselves. Women should know self-defense. Men should know self-defense. It's a skill that could come in handy. God forbid, if they're ever in a situation where they need it, the training will suddenly make a difference. Even it's just enough to land a blow, stun an attacker, and run away. In that scenario, the training, reflexes, and cardiovascular fitness suddenly become a valuable resource.

I think you need to encourage your child to do *something*, to learn to perform, to learn that life is not just sitting on the couch. Even if it's not martial arts. If you're reading this, you're probably the kind of parent who wants your child to be the kind of person who does productive things and self-improves.

And if a martial arts school handles a student the right way, they're going to like it, because it's kind of hard *not* to like it.

Do you get some kids who hate it? Sure. But they hated it before they ever took a lesson. They got it in their mind that they weren't going to like it. You really can't force them to do it. Or you shouldn't. Because that's going to create a rift between you.

If you're determined that your children learn martial arts, sometimes you need to walk them up to it. Sometimes, you need to take an indirect route.

Case Study:

Our operation director's daughter loves dance. Her mother danced for 20 years. Her uncle was a professional ballet dancer, and she loves her uncle.

Dance is great, but his daughter lacked confidence, and they knew martial arts would change her life.

She was afraid to try Taekwondo, because she was terrified of kicking. So we started her in our Tiger Tots youth program.

She loved learning forms, but when it came time to move her to children's class, we knew it would to be a challenge, because of the sparring. Our youth sparring is very low in intensity — it's not *fighting*. Adults can look at it and see it's not dangerous. But for children, it's often a challenge to start their sparring career. Especially when they're in a public arena.

So, he brought the gear home. And they worked at home until she was comfortable. And she could still stay in dance.

As predicted, when she joined the new class, with more drills and new friends, she loved it. The instructor excused her from sparring until she was comfortable. That is a great example of parents and instructors meeting halfway.

chapter 11

"How do I know whether my child is ready to compete?

Question:

"How do I know whether my child is ready to compete?"

Answer:

This is a big question.

For this discussion, when I say "compete," I mean "Olympic-style and/or contact sparring in tournaments." But competing generally falls into one of four categories: sparring, forms, weapons, and breaking.

All four are noble traditions. People have different interests. Some people love forms, and they have zero interest in hitting or being hit, so they don't want to spar. That is fine. Some excellent martial artists do nothing but train on forms, and they are amazing to watch. My daughter Victoria was a great competitor in forms and sparring. You can do both.

Regardless of what area interests you, competition is for people who want to compete, improve aggressively, and perform competitively.

So if your children are interested competing, competing is for them.

If *you* are interested in your child competing, here's the first question to ask: Does your child *want* to compete?

Sparring, weapons, and breaking are all safe when they are conducted in a controlled, professional environment. But especially with sparring, you are potentially putting your child in harm's way. If your child does not want to participate in a contact event, I strongly suggest you don't try to force them into it.

If your child wants to compete, how do you know she is ready?

I like to say "Your instructor will tell you" — but I know our instructors, and I trust their judgment.

So ask yourself: How well does your child do in class? If your child does not spar regularly, he probably needs more experience before he competes in sparring.

At our school, here's how we do it: We set up our own inter-school tournaments that are only open to students from our schools. It's just people we know. Our instructors and students move around enough that even if a student only attends one school, when she arrives at the tournament, she is not surrounded by strangers. It's a bigger building, but it feels like their regular school. There's a comfort level you won't get competing at an open tournament.

Everything is a step at Asian Sun. We set up tournaments so they're building confidence, not ripping it down. Especially at a beginner level.

At interschool tournaments, students can compete in any of four different events: forms, breaking, padded weapons, sparring. So you have four chances to excel.

It's all related. A little taste of success can fix so many of the problems we're talking about: The child doesn't want to go to class. The confidence isn't there. They don't like sparring because they think they're no good. A new form is hard, and the child says, "I can't do it!" Whatever their problem is, if they get a win, if they score a victory, then they have had a taste. People like winning. And now they're on their way.

What tournaments can you enter? Not all tournaments are the same.

If your school offers tournaments, start there. If your school does not host tournaments, ask if they would consider staging one. If your school won't host one, ask your instructor to recommend an outside tournament.

The answer may vary according to a tournament's rules.

Before you enter a tournament, learn about it. Are strikes to the head allowed? Are knockouts allowed in your child's division?

And if they are, are you and your child comfortable with that kind of contact?

Before you enter any tournament, your instructor should evaluate your child. Have your child put on gear and go up against a higher belt. Martial arts are truth in action. If your son feels ready and you think he's great, but he can't defend himself in a controlled environment, then he needs to prepare more before he competes. No question about it.

I'm not saying you have to be technically flawless to enter a competition. But you should have a certain basic defensive competence, especially if it is a full-contact tournament.

The answer can depend on your child's belt level.

For color belts, tournaments have good degree of parity. Divisions will be determined by age, rank, and size. So 13-year-old green belt heavyweights should have a similar level of experience.

For black belt-level competition, the experience and divisions may vary. In a black belt division, you may have an 18-year-old second-degree black belt who has been competing since she was six — and she's going up against your daughter, who might only have four years of martial arts experience, and just joined the competition team after she earned her black belt.

If you are going to an open tournament, ask if an instructor will accompany you. We always have a coach in students' corners at tournaments, whether the event is half an hour away, or on the West Coast. A good coach should improve your results and serve as a safety net.

You don't have to be an elite athlete to have a satisfying, safe competitive experience. You can ease your child into competition.

If you want to compete, you need to manage expectations. We prepare everyone. If it's your first time at Nationals, don't expect to win. It's an amazing experience: People all around, national champions everywhere. But if you expect to win your first national tournament, you're setting yourself up for disappointment. If you get a medal, we'll celebrate that medal, and it will be amazing. But don't expect to win. That's hard to tell students. But it's the truth. It's reality.

Train hard, prepare, and do your best. No matter the outcome, you walk away with experience. Success does not always happen over the course of a single event; success is a process.

Ryan Andrachik and daughter Victoria Ripepi, after winning the grand champion trophy at Master Joe Kim's 2006 North American Challenge.

A favorite motivational quote from Asian Sun Instructor Mike Green:

> "I fear not the man who has practiced 10,000 kicks once. But I fear the man who has practiced one kick 10,000 times."
>
> — Bruce Lee

chapter 12

"My child has special needs, and I'd like him to participate in martial arts, but the condition means he can't do it — right?"

Question:

"My child has special needs, and I'd like him to participate in martial arts, but his condition means he can't do it — right?"

Answer:

Wrong.

Here's the thing with special-needs children. We've been running schools for a long time. We can pretty much instantly identify children with A.D.D., A.D.H.D., and other conditions. We have students with Asperger, students who are legally blind, you name it.

Here's what our approach is: We don't label it. 30 years ago, how many A.D.D. kids were there? I'm not saying it didn't exist — I'm sure it did. But it was never *labeled*.

I have been teaching for 24 years, and I have extensive experience teaching students who have distinct sets of challenges.

I think if your child has special needs or doesn't have special needs, you teach them the same way. You teach them the same thing. If they need to focus, they need to focus. If you have a child who has trouble concentrating now, you don't say, "He *can't* concentrate."

We're going to teach him how to concentrate, but it's not going to happen in a single lesson. Too often, teachers fail to think about *how* people learn. Most people can only absorb so much information at once.

Imagine instructions flowing like water: If I turn on a tap so the water is running nice and slow, you can drink from it. That's how we process instruction: If it comes at a manageable pace, we can take it in.

But if I turn it on the water full blast and tell you to drink, you'll get soaked, and you probably won't be able to take a nice, refreshing, invigorating drink.

If you're not an expert, and I start telling you everything I know, and I correct every little thing, that's like blasting you with a firehose of information. It's overwhelming for any student.

For practically all students, you shouldn't use the firehose approach — especially students with special needs. You start with a slow trickle. And you don't expect to blast away the problem immediately. **It's going to be a process.**

We had two adults who had attended a different school for eight years, and they were red belts. And their old system was never going to let them test for black belt, because the students had special needs, and the instructors were clinging to some old legendary notion like, "Oh, a first degree black belt is a *killer*, and…"

Oh, come on. Be realistic. Their black belt is going to be very different than most other people's black belts. If they can perform the requirements, they might not look the same — but it isn't about everyone being the same.

At any one of our black belt tests, if we have 60 people testing for first degree, a handful will be special-needs, to some degree.

We have a teenager who started with us when he was young, and now he is higher ranking. When he started, he was timid, shy. His parents have still never told us he has special needs. But I can tell — I've been running the school 20 years. His progress has been remarkable. He is more confident. He has developed significant skills. None of us have looked at his needs and decided he has limited potential. If you decide you *can't* do something, you're probably right.

Students with special needs are individuals. All students are. A very intelligent, fully functioning adult student might have limited spatial skills that make it very difficult for him to learn a form. Limitations and special needs aren't always obvious. I know how to read the symptoms. I'm present at all the tests in every school, and I don't just evaluate the students; I evaluate the instructors. So sometimes at a test, a teacher will warn me, "I've been having a really hard time with this student." And I look, and think, "Oh…" and explain it to them. And you can see a light bulb go off over the instructor's head.

When you're learning martial arts, it's all focus and concentration. Special needs or no.

Sometimes, we have a student with severe special needs. Maybe a large, regimented class is not the best environment for them. To start, a student might need private lessons. And who's to say he will always be in a solo class? Regardless, he can learn martial arts. He will benefit from it.

Whether it's school or a dojang, when you are working with a special-needs student, you had better be very creative in how you deal with that child, because you're not dealing with a condition; you're dealing with a personality. So if you can't get through to the child, you lose.

The problem with martial arts in general is: Everyone is so concerned about what they're teaching, they forget about who they're teaching. *What* **you're teaching is nowhere near as important as** *who* **you're teaching.**

And that's what separates the good from the great. There's a book called *Good to Great*, which is about companies that made the leap from being good companies to being great companies. And it's like that with martial arts instructors: Good ones can handle most people. Great ones can handle anybody. And those are few and far between.

Some students who came to us with severe A.D.H.D. went on to become national champions. Children who have A.D.H.D. are a natural fit for martial arts, and here's why: the belt system. It's goal-oriented. You give them a reward for doing a good job, and they're into it. They need to know what's coming next. They *want* to know what's coming next.

Case Study:

We had a student with Asperger Syndrome. We had to change the way we did things with him. Loud noises unsettled him. So when we did line drills, and people were kicking the paddles, every loud pop would just shatter his attention and make him upset.

We didn't take him out of the group class.

Instead, before class, we would take him aside and hit two paddles together, so he could hear the sound and get used to it. Then by the time class started, he was used to the noise, and it didn't bother him.

conclusion

People come to martial arts for one or two ways they want their life to improve — but they end up getting it all.

Anything worth doing in life takes time. As a parent, if your success in your profession came over a long period of time, how can you expect to see changes in your child in one month?

Engaging a martial arts school is engaging a relationship for a long period of time. Please choose wisely.

Thank you for reading!

— Ryan Andrachik, father of four

about asian sun

With nine locations, Asian Sun is Ohio's largest martial arts school. The schools' staff of professional, full-time instructors teach students of all ages Taekwondo, sport Taekwondo, Muay Thai, Krav Maga, Brazilian Jiu-Jitsu, CrossFit, TRX, and fitness kickboxing.

All classes are taught by certified black belt instructors, many of which are past national champions or have coached national champions. Each and every instructor at Asian Sun Martial Arts is handpicked by Grandmaster Andrachik.

Asian Sun instructors are selected from within the Asian Sun Martial Arts organization, and most started with us many years ago, as beginners. They are highly skilled martial artists and motivators. They lead by example and teach with patience and enthusiasm. All of our teachers take a personal interest in every student. They are committed to helping you receive the maximum benefit from your martial arts training.

All Asian Sun instructors are certified through the Asian Martial Arts Council. Asian Sun Martial Arts is registered with USA Taekwondo (the National Governing Body for Taekwondo) and Amateur Athletic Union Taekwondo (AAU).

We teach children how to win at life. Martial arts helps them develop…

• better manners
• respect for parents and other authority figures
• a high degree of self-respect
• a desire to set and achieve goals
• the strength to say "no" to unhealthy peer pressure
• methods to defeat a bully without fighting
• leadership abilities
• a "Yes, I can" attitude
• responsibility for their actions
• better grades in school
• the self-discipline to do what they know they should do without being told
• better concentration skills
• physical and mental self-defense
• better motor skills, coordination, and strength

Over 20 years, Asian Sun has produced 600 black belts, 28 master instructors, and hundreds of national medalists — and contributed to the health and well-being of thousands of great kids and their families.

Facebook.com/AsianSunMartialArts • @Asian_Sun

acknowledgements

I would like to thank the following people for being so influential in my life:

While there are so many people that I need to thank, writing this book would never have happened if it wouldn't have been for the persistent encouragement of David Ferris. Mr. Ferris was so engaging and patient to work with. I always wanted to write this kind of parents' manual, and he has made it possible.

My wife Karen has been not only my biggest supporter, but my partner in all of this. Thank you for your patience, and for telling me what I really meant to say. You always have a way of understanding me.

I need to thank my mom, dad, and grandmother for all of their support. From going to all of my tournaments to paying for lessons, none of this would have been possible without them.

My teacher, Grandmaster Il Joo Kim, certainly had the largest influence on my martial arts career. Grandmaster Kim and Mrs. Kim gave me my first big break with a job — but more than a job, it was a life-changing learning experience. I feel that I learned martial arts and martial arts instruction like the old blacksmiths learned their craft: through on-the-job experience and a lot of tough love. But that is what made me who I am today. I am eternally grateful.

Grandmaster Chaney: Thank you for seeing me as a younger you, and for mentoring me all of these years. I hope that you know how much I appreciate it!

To my children, for giving me *great* material for this book — and also how to improve as an instructor.

The staffs of our Asian Sun and World Kickboxing Academy schools: You accept the fact that we are always striving to produce the best product and service that we can.

Masters Ray and Karen Weinert: I love having you both in my life. Thank you for *always* being there, and for helping me grow and "do the right thing."

— Ryan Andrachik

Youth-division members of Asian Sun's 2013-2014 Competition Team, with Coach Ripepi, at USA Taekwondo's Indiana State Championships, April 2014.

33629860R00064

Made in the USA
Charleston, SC
19 September 2014